ᖅᑲᓗᒃᑐᑦ QIKAALUKTUT

IMAGES OF INUIT LIFE

ᖅᑲᓗᒃᑐᑦ QIKAALUKTUT
IMAGES OF INUIT LIFE

RUTH ANNAQTUUSI TULURIALIK & DAVID F. PELLY

Toronto
OXFORD UNIVERSITY PRESS
1986

CANADIAN CATALOGUING IN PUBLICATION DATA

Tulurialik, Ruth Annaqtuusi, 1934–

  Qikaaluktut : images of Inuit life

ISBN 0-19-540505-6

1. Inuit—Canada—Social life and customs—
Pictorial works.*   2. Tulurialik, Ruth Annaqtuusi,
1934–   I. Pelly, David F. (David Fraser), 1948–
II. Title.

E99.E7T84 1986   971'.00497   C85-099421-7

OXFORD is a trademark of Oxford University Press
Drawings © 1986 Ruth Annaqtuusi Tulurialik
Text © 1986 David F. Pelly
1 2 3 4 5 — 0 9 8 7 6
Printed and bound in Hong Kong by
Scanner Art Services Inc., Toronto

ACKNOWLEDGEMENTS

RUTH ANNAQTUUSI TULURIALIK and DAVID F. PELLY gratefully acknowledge the support of the Explorations Programme of the Canada Council during the preparation of this book; the kindness of Alexis Utatnaq, of Baker Lake, in translating the Introduction by Ruth Annaqtuusi Tulurialik; and the help of the Sanavik Co-operative, Baker Lake, N.W.T., who provided the following drawings for reproduction:
Hungry Kudloopudluakluk
Thunder Sisters
Kazan River
Kingaup Qangani
Imugluqtaq
The Land Gave the People Lots of Food
The Minister

THE PUBLISHERS wish to thank the Inuit Art Section, Indian and Northern Affairs Canada, for photographing the drawings; Nortext Information Design Ltd., Nepean, Ont., who set the Inuktitut syllabics; and The Winnipeg Art Gallery for providing a transparency of *Marble Island*.
Marble Island is reproduced through the courtesy of The Winnipeg Art Gallery:
Ruth Annaqtuusi
Baker Lake (b. 1934)
'Marble Island'
Coloured pencil on paper 56.3 × 76.2 cm
Collection of The Winnipeg Art Gallery.
Acquired with funds donated by Gulf Canada Limited.
Photography: The Winnipeg Art Gallery, Ernest P. Mayer.

ᐱᒪᐊᖅᓂᑊᒪ ᐸᑎ ᐊᓐᐊᖁᖠᕆ
ᑐᓗᕆᐊᓕᑊᒐ ᑎᑎᕋᖅᑕᐅᕐᐊᖠᑊ

ᐱᒥᐊᐊᒍᓄᑎ ᓄᑊᑲᓂ ᑕᐹᖤᑲᐱᐊᐊᒍᑲᐹ. ᒪᐊᑭᑭᐊᐹ-
ᓕᑊ. ᑕᐹᖥᓂ ᡰᐊᕆ ᐹᓝᐄ ᐊᕆᖤᑲᓕᐹᑊᒐ ᑎᑎᓕᐹ-
ᖥᓂᒐ ᑕᕝ ᑎᑎᕋᐹᕒᕝᖤᑕ Lᓷ. ᓬᓲᒍᑊᑲᑊᓕ ᐅᑐ-
ᑊᒥᐃᒐ 1965ᒐ—ᐊᐹᑊᕰᓲᐊᐱᑊᓲᐃ.

ᐃᕆᓕᑕᑐᑎᑲᐹᐃᐃ ᐅᓂᑊᑲᐹᑊ ᑎᑎᕿᐸᑲᑊ ᑲᓂᓲᑊᑊ
ᐅᒥᑭᐊᓲᐊ ᑲᑐᐊ ᑕᕷᓬᐅᑐ ᐊᐽ ᓄᑊᕷᑊ ᑐᑊᕼᑲᓲᐊᓕᑊ
ᐃᕼᓲᑭᓲᓂ. ᑎᐹ ᐱᑊ ᐃᑲᕳᕒᐊᑲᐹᑊ ᐅᓂᑊᑲᐊᑲᐹᑎᓓᐊᓕ
ᒍᐱᐊᕷᓲᒥᕝᕝᑕ ᑎᐊᐊᐃᑐᑭᕒᕝᐹᕝᑊ ᑲᐹᕳᕝᕝᑕᕝ ᐃᑲᕷᑎᑊ-
ᕝᐊᑲᐹᑲ ᑲᐊᐊ ᐃᑲᕼᕝᐊᑲᐹᑊ.

ᐃᑊᑎᕷᕒᒐᕒᑕ ᐃᑊᐄ ᑲᑊᒍᒐ ᑐᑊᕷᕼᐊᑲᐹᑊ ᑎᑎᕿᐹ-
ᕷᕇᕳᕼᑊ ᑐᑊᕷᑊᕷᕉ ᕷᓲᐹᕝᕝᑕ Lᑊᑊ ᑐᑊᕷᕷᑊᕼᑕᓂ.

ᑕᕝᑭᐊ ᐅᓂᑊᑲᐹᐊ ᐅᑲᑊᕷᑊᕒᕝᕝᕝᑕ ᑕᐹᕷᕼᑊᐊ Lᓲᒐ
ᓂᑊᕳᒐ. ᑲᑲᑊᒐ ᑕᐽᓲᐊᑲᑲ ᖤᑊᓲᑐᑊ ᐃᕝ ᑲᑭᐊ ᐅᓲ-
ᑲᑭᐊ ᑎᑎᕿᐸᕷᕳᐊᓲ ᐃᑊᕳ ᖤᑊᓲᓲᐊᐹᓲᕝᕝᕝᕳ.

ᖦᕳᓲᑭᐊᖥ. ᓄᓓᑊᕳᐊᖥ
ᕳᓲ 1985

ᐸᑎ ᐊᓐᐊᖁᖠᕆ ᑐᓗᕆᐊᓕᑊ   Ruth Annaqtuusi Tulurialik

INTRODUCTION
by Ruth Annaqtuusi Tulurialik

My first drawings, as a child, were just pages of faces. But other children enjoyed looking at them. A long time ago Jessie Oonark taught me about drawing; that's why I can draw a little bit now. Somebody told me I started drawing seriously in 1965—I don't remember.

For a long time I have wanted to combine stories with my drawings so people down south—and my own children—could understand the scenes from our old ways. When I learned that my friend David Pelly was a writer I asked him to help me. I am very happy that he agreed. He has put a lot of energy into the book. I could sense his excitement as we worked together.

Though the stories are not written here in Inuktitut, I think older Inuit readers will understand the drawings. They will recognize many things that younger people do not know about.

These are stories passed down to me by our people. We called the collection *Qikaaluktut* because for me the stories and drawings are like those sounds.

Baker Lake, N.W.T.
June 1985

INTRODUCTION
by David F. Pelly

For five days in mid-April 1983 I was stuck, together with Tulurialik, in an iglu at Kamanaqyuk, which means something like 'nice little bay'. On the last day of the fox-trapping season we had headed out on the land from Baker Lake, an Inuit community in the Northwest Territories. A storm began on our first night. For four days it blew a blizzard of proportions I had never imagined. In the dim light of the iglu (the icy walls were translucent) we played string games, drank tea, finished our meagre food supplies, talked occasionally, learned from each other, peered outside through a crack between two snow blocks at impenetrable whiteness . . . and became good friends.

Back in Baker Lake I spent a lot of time in Tulurialik's house, just visiting, a major activity in the North. His wife Ruth always gave me tea, even when I didn't ask for it. I recognized her as the dishwasher from the hotel. The previous summer, on my first visit to Baker Lake, I lived in a tent near the hotel and the friendly manager offered me lots of coffee, some leftover cakes, and the occasional shower. I always got a big smile from the lady who was silently collecting and washing the dishes. I smiled back, but we ended that summer in silence. Ruth doesn't remember me from the hotel. She smiles at everyone.

Not long after my introduction to waiting out a blizzard on the land, Tulurialik, Ruth, and I were sitting at their kitchen table drinking tea. Out of the blue she said, 'You're a writer. Will you help me with my book?'

Shortly thereafter she showed me the drawings she had been collecting in her back room—a year's work waiting for the right opportunity to put them into a book, with their stories. In the following days I learned that this smiling dishwasher was one of the most important Inuit artists in Canada, known in the art world as Annaqtuusi.

* * *

Ruth was born in 1934 on a small island in the Kazan River, which flows into the south side of Baker Lake, 200 miles to the west of Hudson Bay. At birth she was given the name Annaqtuusi, after an ancestor of her mother, Martha Talerook. As an infant, Ruth was adopted by Thomas and Elizabeth Tapatai. They lived at the Anglican mission, amid the small cluster of buildings erected by the Hudson's Bay Company, the RCMP, and the Roman Catholic mission on the northwest shore of the lake. Since that time Ruth has seen the settlement become Baker Lake, a community of approximately 1,000 people—the only Inuit community in the North not on the sea. In the late 1950s she married Hugh Tulurialik, a strong, good-humoured hunter. They have three children.

With the establishment of the Baker Lake Sanavik Cooperative in 1970, which provided paper and coloured pencils, Ruth was encouraged to draw. Her drawings were translated into prints that were included in the Baker Lake annual collections of 1971, '72, '73, and most years since. However, the complexity of lines and colours renders her drawings difficult to reproduce by stone-cut and stencil. A much larger body of work is presented here showing scenes from traditional life, and legends, depicted with great imagination and energy. These photographic reproductions are all from the original drawings.

The people about whose way of life Ruth is drawing —and, in this book, speaking—are chiefly the inland Inuit, dwellers of the Barren Lands, people for whom the caribou were fundamental to life. Removed from the sea and its bounty, they depended upon caribou for food, clothing, shelter, transportation, and tools. They lived in one of the world's harshest environments. In the late 1950s these people of the Barrens were decimated by starvation. The survivors then began to live in settlements, one of which was Baker Lake.

*   *   *

One day I sat at Ruth's kitchen table and watched as she began a new drawing. She stared at the blank paper for a few minutes, hand poised, plain lead pencil only a millimetre off the surface, clearly deep in thought. Then she drew two tiny eyes, which were soon encompassed by the body of a woman. Then a second figure began to take shape beside the first.

'My head is fast; my hands are slow,' Ruth complained.

I left her in peace to draw. When I returned the scene was fully sketched: two iglus full of people and several other figures outside, all depicting a birth in camp. The colour was added with pencils. When she was finished, Ruth told me the story behind her picture.

We always discussed her drawings amidst much drinking of tea, laughter, and external interruptions. Ruth spoke to me in simple English, sprinkling her discourse with many Inuktitut words that were familiar to me. Often while sitting over a drawing she would giggle, amused by the sight of her own inventiveness: a seal walking on land, an unmarried man using a woman's ulu, a polar bear helping to carry a kayak.

*   *   *

Qikaaluktut—that is what Ruth called this collection. When I asked her the meaning of the word, she said that it referred to 'the sounds of people passing by, perhaps outside your iglu, heard but not seen.' For Ruth her drawings, and the stories she tells about them, are like those sounds.

I worked with Ruth on each story until I knew I understood all the shades of her meaning. I wanted to help her achieve her aims, one of which was 'to teach the qablunat about the old ways'. However, I did not see my role as an interpreter of her graphic symbolism.

So much has been written about the North from a southern perspective that this text had to be different. Ruth is talking to you, the reader, directly. She is telling you her own story and the story of her people. It is an irreplaceable record of a way of life on which history has turned the page. Ruth once said to me: 'Even my own children don't know how we lived when I was young.'

GLOSSARY

These Inuktitut words, many of which are used more than once in the text that follows, are defined only after their first mention.

amauti, baby's pouch on the back of an *atigi*
atigi, light inner parka
atqut, tool for trimming lampwicks
auladjut, bone jigger with line for fishing
iglu, snow house
inuk, man, person
inuksuk, pile of rocks ('likeness of man')
Inuit, 'the people', 'mankind'
Inuktitut, the Inuit language
iqtuqsit, scraper
japa, cloth parka
kakinniq, tattoos
kakivak, fish spear
kamiik, pair of skin boots
kyppak, a particular style of parka
nanuit, polar bears
nanuq, polar bear
naqturalik, eagle
pissiq, song
pualrit, wooden snow shovel

puluatsit, smoking-pipe
qablunaq, white man
qablunat, white men
qamutik, sled
qariariit, iglu with three chambers
qarliik, caribou pants
qattaq, caribou-skin water bucket ('for carrying water')
qilaujaniq, drum dance
qingumigvik, a pile of rocks on which you can rest your telescope when looking for caribou
qulittaq, caribou-skin parka
qulliq, oil lamp
sakuut, scraper
sik-sik, ground squirrel
tukipqutaq, rock on top of an *inuksuk*, pointing to a good fishing place
tuktu, caribou
ukpik, owl
ulu, woman's knife
umingmak, musk-ox

FOR QAUMANAAQ

When I was very young I went fishing through the ice with my mother, Elizabeth Tapatai. It was a spring day when I caught my first fish, in Baker Lake. An old lady, Qaumanaaq, sewed the fish-tail on my japa (cloth parka), as a sign so everyone would know right away when they saw me. It had to be done by someone who was not a relative. People do not do this now. Nobody knows anymore. Only old people, they know. Old Qaumanaaq died a long time ago when I was a child. The fish-tail she sewed on my japa lasted only a week or so before it fell off somewhere. But I do not forget her.

A long time ago people knew it was important. The evening when the young boy in the green atigi (light inner parka) caught a fish, his first, the fins were cut off to be sewn on his atigi. He was fishing with his sister and mother, while his father chopped a new hole for his own sister, whose family was travelling with them. Her husband is building a snow shelter for another fishing hole. It is November and these two families have just arrived in the camp, where they will stay for the winter.

A father, mother, and two sons have been living in this camp for a month and are happy to see these new people. The man is telling his wife that she must sew the fish-tail for the young boy so that he will always have good luck in fishing. As he speaks he thinks of the fish-tail, and his wife thinks of the tail moving from the fish to the boy and becoming attached to the arms of his atigi.

The qariariit (iglu with three chambers) was built in October with the first good snow. There is room enough for all the new arrivals, but they will build their own iglu in the days ahead. The main room of the iglu is made comfortable for the long winter, with snow piled up outside the walls for warmth. There is also an ice window and a chimney. Do you see the extra snow block on the top? It has a hole through the middle. Without this, the air hole would melt and become too big.

These people always recognized the first fish of a child. Many people today have never heard of this old way. I feel better inside to make a drawing of it. We should pay attention to some of the ideas of the old people.

HUNGRY KUDLOOPUDLUAKLUK

The Kudloopudluakluk is a sea creature, of no particular form, who lives beneath the waters. I think of the monster as having many faces. We children were warned by the older people not to play too close to the water for fear of being caught. In October, when the ice is not too thick, we were scared because we could hear the Kudloo-pudluakluk moving under the ice. He was not always bad. But you could never tell for sure, so we stayed away.

This monster is a hungry one, attacking the big fish. The children can hear him under the ice and they are scared.

THE FISHING HOLE

In October, before the ice is very thick, it is quite easy to chop a hole. One man wanted some fresh water, so he made a hole. But another man decided to fish there. He caught one right away and his wife is excited, waiting to cut it up because they have had nothing to eat for three days. The first man is watching for more fish through the ice, ready to spear one with his kakivak (fish spear) as it passes under the hole. No one has noticed the nanuq (polar bear) yet. He would also like to have a fish. Even the young boy, who is not at the fishing hole, has not seen the nanuq because he is busy hunting birds with a sling-shot.

The two oldest sons from each family have gone out hunting together far away from camp. They are now one day's travel away. Earlier they killed a caribou, and now one of them has just caught an umingmak (musk-ox). Soon there will be lots of food in camp.

NEW CAMP

When people came to a new camp there was always lots to do. These two families have just arrived. One of the men is building an iglu. His daughter is helping by using a pualrit (wooden shovel) to pile snow around the outside. His wife has chopped a hole through the ice, often thicker than a man's height, and built a small shelter for fishing. Beside her on the ice is her ulu (woman's knife). She is using an auladjut, made of bone, for jigging. So far she has two fish. But the dogs are stealing the fish and looking very pleased about it.

Their son, in the green atigi, is helping the other woman hunt a caribou bull. A long time ago people could stalk right up to caribou and kill them with a snow knife. Soon these two families will have meat and fish to eat in their new iglu.

But there is trouble. The other father, in the purple atigi, is calling to his fourteen-year old son, telling him to lie very still. There is a nanuq. The son is pretending to be dead, while his father prepares to shoot the bear with a carefully aimed arrow. They say that if a nanuq comes near you, the best thing to do is to lie perfectly still. He will not attack if he thinks you are dead. He is only interested if you are alive.

We heard a true story about playing dead for a nanuq from Jimmy Mukpa, the Inuk Anglican minister in Eskimo Point. He was out hunting a few years ago, in the summer, with another man. They were sleeping under their up-turned boat. A nanuq came. Both of their rifles were out of reach, so they did not move. The bear put his front paws on the canoe. One man had the seat of the boat across his chest, so he had to support this weight without moving or saying anything. They could hardly breathe. They knew if they moved they would be attacked by the nanuq. Eventually the bear went away.

NEW IGLU

The new iglu will be very bright inside, even though it is
the dark time of year, just before Christmas. The stars shine
brightly, and a thin crescent moon lights up the snow. This is
to be the new camp for a family who just arrived. Father is
completing their iglu, while his wife uses her pualrit to
throw loose snow around the outside. Their son is running toward the new iglu, frightened by a nanuq. Their
dogs are barking.

   In the midst of the excitement two other families have
just arrived from another direction. One man is going to
kill the nanuq, while his wife prepares to cut up a seal he
caught earlier. These visitors will stay in camp overnight,
sharing the new iglu, then continue on their way to a new
place. But they will be back. For Christmas is soon, and
this is to be the camp where families from all around will
gather to celebrate in the new iglu.

CHRISTMAS

A long time ago all the people came together during Christmas month. In those days they knew about God and Jesus but did not understand what it all meant. When the first people arrived at the gathering place they built an iglu big enough for everyone. Three people are now putting the finishing touches on the iglu: one lady working with a pualrit and one man fixing the ice window. Inside there are lots of people, represented by the large, smiling faces across the back. In front are all the things they have in the iglu with them: kakivak, arrow, sling used for hunting birds, puluatsit (smoking pipe), atqut (tool for trimming lampwicks), qulliq (oil lamp), pualrit, snowknife, ulu, sakuut (scraper), bow and arrow, auladjut—lots of things. Everything is ready for the arrival of a great hunter and his wife, the last people to come, bringing with them some meat cached earlier for the Christmas celebration. This special man is respected, admired, and feared by the other people because he is so strong, such a great hunter. When he arrives he will signal, by both his presence and his supply of meat, that the celebration shall begin.

BIRTH

This is an important moment in a winter camp. It is early morning. A woman in the big iglu is about to give birth. An older woman has been with the pregnant woman during her labour all night. She is a 'doctor' (mid-wife). Certain elders were known for this skill. My mother helped many women give birth.

Everything is organized. The children have been sent outside to play. A young girl is running to a neighbouring iglu to call another elder to help with the birth. The woman's husband is putting on his qarliik (caribou pants) before leaving the iglu while the birth is taking place. Some women like many people with them. Others are like me and want to be just with the elders.

After the baby is born the women helping always put a finger down the mother's throat to try to make her vomit. That's the Inuit way. The baby is cleaned up, and the 'doctor' immediately rubs the baby's soft misshapen head into a normal form, then gives it to the mother for feeding. Soon after, the father will come back into the iglu to see his child.

The parents have already picked a name, which they give to the child right away. Names do not tell the child's sex. The name comes from an old relative, even a dead one.

You see a woman telling her pregnant daughter-in-law that she should go outside early every morning to check the weather. That is the Inuit way. A pregnant woman should continue her routine, like the woman at the top. Then she will have an easier labour.

The elders' opinions should always be heeded. The husband's father sees his son holding just one fox when he should have about nine. He says his son is not paying attention to his hunting and trapping because his wife is pregnant. The elders are important to young couples having children. They give help and advice.

KIIQTURTUT

The woman in the centre of the big iglu is having a difficult time giving birth. So all the other women, who are 'doctors', are with her. They take turns holding her hand and helping her, while the others perform Kiiqturtut, walking in a circle around the pregnant woman. She is on a bed of caribou skins laid on top of willow branches to make the bed soft and dry. As they walk, the women chant something like *Hi, Hi, Hi, Hi* . . . This is only done for a woman who has a hard labour. Some go on all night and all day!

Some births are easier. The woman in the small iglu had an easy labour. She gave birth on her own, without any help. The baby is now wrapped in caribou skin. The mother is able to continue her routine, using the qulliq to heat water for tea and to dry out some wet kamiik (pair of skin boots).

Another baby boy, born a few days ago, is receiving a caribou hat made by a woman who is saying that he will be a really good hunter. The woman is thinking of all the animals he will hunt. This ceremony was important. People still give gifts like this today, but the same ideas do not go with them.

A little boy is beginning to learn the skills of a hunter from his father. They hide behind a qingumigvik (pile of rocks) to look for caribou.

Life starts out in different ways, sometimes hard and sometimes easier. But for a boy it is always the same—learning to be a good hunter.

DEATH

Two hunters, about to leave their camp to go in search of caribou for their hungry families, talk about death, which is part of their life. They must find food or their people will die. They talk about making a shelter in which to eat while they are hunting, or one of them might die.

In another camp, far away, a young boy has just died. Maybe he was sick. His father, in the purple atigi, looks on as two men place the child in his grave—a box sitting on the ground, encircled by an oval ring of small stones to mark the site. The two men, 'the workers' who arrange the surface grave, wear old kamiik and mitts. After the job is done these old items of clothing will be burned in a fire, discarded forever.

Two women in the camp are agreeing not to eat any marrow, a favourite food, so soon after the boy died. People tried not to break any bones for about ten days after somebody died. So the women holding the caribou legs cannot smash the bones to get at the marrow.

An older man in camp instructs a young boy to go to a nearby camp where there are some old people, who must be told of the death. It is his job to carry the news.

Otherwise life continues normally.

PLAYING GAMES

Games were played at any time of year, by both adults and children. Some were competitions; others were played for fun.

In *Sitorktaq* the people crouch and kick out one leg, then the other. The person who continues kicking the longest is the winner.

Ayagak is a quiet game of skill. On one end of a piece of sinew a hollowed caribou bone is tied, and on the other an antler tip. The player must swing the bone into the air and try to spear it with the antler tip. It is not easy.

Arm wrestling is another game. Who is stronger?

Throat singing is often part of a celebration. Two women chant together, but it is not a competition.

The head pull and foot pull are other tests of strength. You pull your opponent over a line. Here a woman has just lost a foot pull while her husband looks on.

All these games are still played today.

FLYING SHAMAN

A shaman could do anything. This one is a woman—you can tell because she is wearing women's qarliik and has strings for an amauti (baby's pouch on an atigi). She is flying, carrying all these people to a new camp. The rest of the people, left behind in the old camp, are having a drum dance because they know that the next day they will be following their friends, with a different shaman. They are all happy to leave because they have been hungry in this camp. The shaman has found a new camp where there is lots of food.

Maybe this never happened.

OLD LADY

This old lady is a shaman. The birds all around are her spirits. She is decorated in the old way, with kakinniq (tattoos), as women used to be. A long time ago women had these thin black lines on their faces, thighs, and hands. They were made by passing a caribou needle, rubbed in the charcoal of a fire, under the upper layers of the skin. The lines were considered beautiful.

REGIONAL Ꭰꭰ Ꭰꮃ Ꭰꮃ
RUTH TULURIALIK

SHAMAN GRANDMOTHER BRINGS FOOD

The shaman has been dead a long time. Her relatives, her daughter's family, were hungry in their camp beside this swift-flowing river. So the shaman returned, together with a spirit who helped her, to see that her descendants were given food. They caught fish. The father caught a caribou, and his wife will soon be making dried meat. Nobody can see the shaman, but she has made the food come.

The shaman's visit also brings good fortune for two men who happen to be passing by. They too will enjoy good fishing now. The shaman's benevolence extends beyond her family. A young boy in the light-green atigi will join the two travellers in their large kayaks to go hunting. He wants to take two baby nanuit (polar bears) with him. His father and two other sons will also share in the good fish-ing with their friends in camp. There will be no more hunger in this camp after the shaman's visit.

Shamans were not always invisible. Some, both men and women, lived in Baker Lake when I was young. That is what I heard. I never knew who they were. They were supposed to be able to do anything. Two islands near here are special places for shamans. When people stayed there overnight, in the morning they found something missing—equipment, dogs, anything. One man did not believe in shamans and he went out to camp on these islands. In the morning he found his dog lying dead.

Shamans are no longer part of our life in the settlement. But everyone is still afraid of the spirits from past shamans, who might be out on their islands.

THROWING PEOPLE INTO THE AIR

A shaman can use special powers just for playing. The woman carrying a child in her amauti is a shaman. Just for fun she has used her kakivak to toss her friends up in the air—a husband and his wife, who is holding a fish she just caught. This makes the shaman laugh, causes her husband to speak, but frightens the young boy in the green atigi, who has never seen anyone do such a thing before. And with only one hand—such strength!

The young boy, now running, is dragging back to camp a seal his father caught earlier. His father, in the qulittaq (caribou-skin parka), is also a shaman, but he caught this seal as an ordinary hunter. Now he is using his special magic to hold up nanuq for his friend to shoot. He does this without the hunter knowing he is being helped, for only the shaman knows that he is holding the bear, and he thinks of the arrow that will kill the bear.

All these people live in the same camp. It is spring and they have lots of food, so it is a happy place—a camp where the shamans can also play.

THUNDER SISTERS

This is the old Inuit story of how thunder began.

Two young girls were orphans. They were afraid of their step-parents and other people. They thought of turning into animals to escape from them. The younger girl suggested wolves, lemmings, birds, wondering which would be safer. But her older sister said no, because if they were animals they would be caught by the hunters. Finally they thought of becoming the makers of thunder, because in the sky they would be safe from hunters' arrows and spears.

They went up into the sky, riding on a caribou skin with the fur scraped off. Now they make thunder, each sitting on a dark cloud high in the sky, with the caribou skin stretched between them. The sound of thunder is really two noises, one slightly lower than the other. Each sister makes one of these sounds.

The older people are offering coloured beads to the rain clouds because they are afraid of the revenge of the thunder sisters for being treated badly.

MARBLE ISLAND

I heard the story of Marble Island from my uncle, Titus Seeteenak. This island of white stone, in Hudson Bay near Rankin Inlet, was originally ice floating in the sea. But it sat there so long it turned to stone. Many people died there, both Inuit and qablunat (white men). The old tradition says that the first time you go there you have to crawl up onto the land. When you reach the high-water tide mark you can stand up and walk.

All these people are crawling because it is their first time on Marble Island. They came by kayak. The man standing in the middle is yelling, telling the others by the shore that they must crawl in order not to offend the spirits that dwell on the island. A ship is sailing into the bay where the whalers used to winter over; the man with the big hat is a trader bringing tea. Earlier there was a shipwreck and some qablunat were stuck on the island to die. You can still see their graves.

Marble Island is a magic place.

KAUJAJU'S STORY

I heard this story about two men a long time ago.

One man, named Kivigajuga, which means 'pants almost off', came to visit a famous man, Kaujaju. But when he entered the iglu, Kaujaju threw him back into the porch with the dogs. This scene is shown in the bigger iglu, with the words 'Kaujaju throwing out Kivigajuga' telling the story. Kaujaju's two wives are looking on.

Somehow, we don't know how, Kivigajuga takes over the iglu and throws out Kaujaju, who goes to seek comfort from a friendly nanuq. The lower iglu, really the same one, shows the outcome as Kivigajuga now sits in his iglu with a nanuq he has killed. The words beside him— 'Kivigajuga has the iglu now *and* a nanuq, food for a whole year'—complete the story.

AULLAAQTUT—MOVING AWAY

Families had to move when there was no food. The second oldest son in this family, maybe 17, wearing the brown atigi and carrying a heavy pack, has just returned to camp after three days of hunting. The father chose him to go searching because he was the best hunter of the sons—it is not always the eldest who learns those skills the fastest. He brings a report of tuktu (caribou) only two days away.

Before leaving, the family has just eaten the remaining supply of dried fish—one of the sons is finishing up their last fish. The boys are still hungry, so hungry they are trying to catch a sik-sik (ground squirrel), the only animal left near the old camp. One of them is throwing stones, another is shooting with bow and arrow, and one is trying to trap the sik-sik with a lasso of a caribou sinew.

Everything is packed onto the dog and the father's back. The youngest son is too weak to walk so he is also on his father's shoulders. His wife is in front of him, with their first daughter in her amauti, guiding her tired husband by the hand. In these times they always help each other. They must now walk for two days, looking for animals as they travel. It is very warm, with lots of mosquitoes.

But in the new camp they will make lots of dried fish. And when the hunt is successful there will be meat to cache for the winter. That is the hope that keeps them going.

*   *   *

I want you to hear my husband's story. He was very young when his family moved from Schultz Lake north to the Back River, a distance of nearly 150 miles. He was the only child in his family. There were also his parents, his grandmother, an uncle and his wife. This is his story:

We moved to the Back River because there were no caribou and not very good fishing where we were. We were following another family and were behind them maybe two days. They knew the way to go to the Back River, to a good fishing place. I do not think my uncle and my father knew exactly about this place. So we were following their tracks in early spring, maybe April. It was not too cold, but snowing.

I do not know how many dogs we had, something like four or five, enough to pull the sled easily. Before we reached there, two or three of our dogs died of hunger. We kept following the tracks, travelling at night because it was colder, and easier to pull the sled.

Finally we reached the family at their new camp beside Garry Lake on the Back River. They were only two days ahead of us but they already had lots of fish. I was cold and hungry, but they just let me have a little bit of fish, because they did not want to feed me. I had been hungry for at least three days, about a week maybe. They put me in bed right away because I was cold.

Very early next morning, when everyone was sleeping, my grandmother woke me up and told me to do some fishing. I got dressed, went on the ice not far from the tent, and started fishing. As soon as the hook went into the water in the hole, a fish bit it. I took it up to the tent right away. Then I went back to the hole. I caught another fish and took it to the tent. Then back down again. I went back and forth, with one fish each time, because I was a child.

When everybody got up that morning of our first day in the new camp, there were lots and lots of fish. I remember that well!

FAMILY TRAVELS

This family left their winter camp, a long way away, because there was no food. It is a happy time, when the ice is gone, maybe in June or July, because they are moving to where there are more animals and more fish.

All the food they had to bring with them was two seals, tied onto the kayaks. In this time they did not eat any qablunat food, only fish and seal and caribou. They travel in five kayaks made of caribou skin. The parents are in one together, with their dog, and four sons are in the others, the eldest leading, so that the younger sons can watch their older brothers and learn from them.

After travelling for three days they are arriving at the mouth of a dangerous river where they will camp for the summer, because the fast water means good fishing. Already as they approach, the second son in the dark green japa is using his kakivak. But the mother is holding onto her husband; she is scared a bit by the current. The youngest son, maybe 23, in the light green japa, is having trouble with the current because it is his first year to be in his own kayak. Last year he rode with one of his older brothers.

In three months, after a summer of fishing, the family will return to their winter camp, with the kayak full of dried fish. Then next spring the search will begin again for a good fishing place to spend the summer.

FIGHTING

A family is ready to leave camp. They have no more food. Before they go the eldest son has gone fishing for something to eat as they travel. While they wait for his return the man and his wife happily juggle some stones. Their youngest son, in caribou-skin clothing, plays on his own.

Another family, father and two sons, also live in this camp. They have decided to stay, and fortunately the two boys have just found a nanuq to provide them with meat.

A strange man who has just arrived is not a welcome visitor. He is quarrelling with the man of the camp, saying, 'You are not very strong!' This angers the father, so he is determined to send this man away. Sometimes people start fighting in play and then get angry for real . . . and end up fighting.

HUNGRY PEOPLE

In 1958, when I was working at the nursing station, I remember some hungry people coming there for food. In the camps out on the land sometimes there was no food. Some people were so hungry they could not walk for help; they just sat there waiting to die. Many people died.

In the settlement there was a man from Indian and Northern Affairs with a plane. He went out to the camps and brought people into the settlement. There was an old cabin along the shore near the airstrip where they kept the dead people, sometimes frozen.

People who came into the settlement then usually built iglus here and stayed. They never returned to the land.

I heard stories like these from people arriving in the settlement from the camps:

An old couple who have some food have sent two children to walk to another camp where there are some hungry people, to ask them to come and share the food. The old woman has some caribou in her iglu and her husband has just caught a fish. He is so hungry he immediately starts to eat it.

One man walking along was so hungry that he fell down. Now he is thinking of his wife and child.

A woman is making a thin soup by boiling a caribou skin.

Another woman is trying to feed her husband something by scraping a caribou skin.

Two boys are going fishing. One of them has caught a ptarmigan.

Four women, sitting in their iglu with no food, are so hungry they cannot walk. A man is trying to catch a bird for them to eat.

TUKIPQUTAQ

The tukipqutaq is a rock that marks a place where the fishing is very good. It is placed on top of an inuksuk (pile of rocks) and its special shape points out over the water. If you look along the top of the stone you can see where the fish are. A man from a camp near this inuksuk is out hunting a caribou that was trying to cross the river, while his son fishes from the point.

Another family is travelling with the strong spring current down the river. They know about this fishing place from years past so have planned to stop before continuing the journey. The oldest son, in the lead, has already reached the spot indicated by the tukipqutaq and is readying his kakivak and auladjut. The rest of the family are not far behind in their kayaks, the father accompanied by the youngest son, the mother keeping an eye on the next son. This is his first time travelling in his own kayak and he is having some trouble with the current. So he is walking his kayak through the shallow water. He will soon rest on shore.

The family will be on its way in a few hours, thankful the tukipqutaq has once again provided them with a good supply of fish for the journey ahead.

SUNSET

These three familes left their winter camp to travel to a
new camp. As evening fell and the sun began to set they
came across an old inuksuk. They had never been this way
before, so they were excited when they saw the tukipqutaq,
pointing to a good fishing place.

Already they have lots of fish. One family is just landing
on the beach. Their youngest son has run ahead to start
fishing beside the inuksuk, using a bone auladjut for jigging. His father must explain to him the meaning of the
tukipqutaq. The second son, in the purple atigi, waded
ashore to help bring the kayak in. Wearing kamiik made
of caribou skin with all the fur scraped off, he will never
get his feet wet. The oldest brother is guiding the kayak in,
while his father stands at the back to help. Both of them
are smoking old pipes, a wooden stem with a hollowed-
out stone for a bowl. They smoke small green leaves picked
from the ground.

Two other families are out in their kayaks fishing. A mother and father are using the kakivak to catch so many fish
their son is joyful. They are towing another kayak because
there wasn't enough wood to make another paddle. In this
smaller kayak are two of three sons belonging to a widow.
She is the woman with the big ulu, watching over her sons.

They will stay here to fish. It is a good time while the
sun goes down. Then their journey will continue, with
lots of fish tied to the kayaks. That will surely be food
enough to take them to the next tukipqutaq.

CROSSING THE WATER

All these people are travelling together over the land a long time ago. They do not have many kayaks, so crossing the river is not easy. Two men are carrying six children on a kakivak so they will not get their feet wet. The women are already across and are watching from the far shore. I think this is just an idea from my imagination. I never heard it as a real story.

Regional

ᑭᓇ ᓴᓇᖅ

Ruth Tulurialik

KAZAN RIVER

The Kazan River, where I was born, has a lot of islands where the water goes quickly past. Many people are travelling on the river. One family is going downstream, the father paddling, the oldest son hunting, and the mother running along the shore holding the kayak by a rope. Other people in their kayaks are troubled by the swift current swirling by the end of the island. A woman on the point of the island has two coils of seal sinew, used as ropes. She wants to help catch the caribou.

   On the island in the middle of all these travellers, a man and woman in their camp are having a drum dance. She seems very happy.

KINGAUP QANGANI—
ON TOP OF THE HILL

The man on top of the hill, looking through his telescope from behind the rocks, says that he sees many hundred tuktu. His wife is coming with bow and arrow to hunt for some fresh meat.

In the camp below there is a lot of activity, typical of a clear day in the winter. A woman is fishing, children are running in play, a man is hunting nanuq, another man is going fishing. A traveller has just arrived in the camp, where he will stay with these people. He has no dogs, so he must pull his own qamutik (sled).

The words in the camp explain that years ago people said if we left our kamiik standing up by themselves, or left a pualrit stuck upright in the snow, they would walk away by themselves while we slept.

MAN CARRYING CARIBOU

It is springtime—a good time, but very hot. The man must work hard to carry all the meat, covered with a skin, from the caribou he caught earlier today. They have travelled a long way. His young daughter is too tired to walk, so he must carry her too. And the youngest son is walking slowly beside his father. The second son is trying to kill another caribou. After a few more hours of walking, they will find their camp.

Their oldest son went hunting on his own for the day, in the opposite direction from his father. He too has had success, finding a nanuq.

Spring is a time of plenty. But it is a time when land travel is hard. A man must not only find the meat. He must carry it on his back to his family's camp.

IMIGLUQTAQ

It was a nice day. But then it started raining and a rainbow formed. A man on a nearby hilltop is raising his arms like antlers signalling that he sees tuktu.

In the camp below people are talking. The woman on the left in the yellow atigi is talking to her husband as she plays with an imigluqtaq, a piece of caribou skin on a length of a sinew that makes a whistling noise. 'I am sorry to be playing with imigluqtaq,' she says, 'but I am bored.' Her husband is angry because her noise is bringing bad weather when a lot of hunters want to go out after tuktu.

She answers, 'Whoever was born in the summer should take off their atigi so the weather will not change,' in keeping with Inuit tradition. Their son hears this and runs off through camp yelling, 'Somebody should come out without their atigi so the weather will be good.'

A man comes out of the caribou-skin tent wearing no atigi. While he scratches his bare stomach, he shouts at the weather to be good.

RIVER IN SPRING

When the river opens in June there is a happy feeling of new beginnings. Nature comes to life again, the current flows swiftly. The people are full of life, fighting just for fun, while off to one side a father is teaching his son the qilaujaniq (drum dance). He has just made the boy, about 14, his first caribou-skin drum. The son asks, 'How do you do this?'

Another family passes by in their kayaks: father, son, and mother. They are brave to chance the fast current. But it will carry them downriver to a new camp, a place for a new beginning.

FISHING AT SUNRISE

Two kayaks are on their way to the river mouth. Even as they near the ocean the fishing is good. There are lots of fish—for Inuit, nanuit, and the grizzly bear.

Regional ᐳᓐᔪᐊᕐᒥ
Ruth Tulurialik

COMING TOGETHER IN THE SPRING

All these families have gathered in this spring camp. This was the place where they agreed to meet. Some families have brought more meat than others, to be shared around the group. Some have had help from the friendly fish in their travelling to get here. Now everyone is happy. To celebrate the coming together of friends, one man is doing a qilaujaniq, with his wife chanting 'Ai ya ya . . . ' beside him.

All around the camp people are joining in the celebration, watching the dance or doing other things. One man just caught a fish, which his wife is ready to cut up with her ulu. Two boys are walking on their hands, while a girl tries unsuccessfully to do the same but falls down laughing. One man is shouting that he has a kayak somewhere and is going to get it. Soon the families will travel together to a new summer camp.

A HAPPY CAMP

In a spring camp, when everything is going well, the fishing is good and there are lots of animals, it is a happy time. It makes me think of funny things, like seals walking on the land. This unmarried man is using a woman's ulu, as he calls out to his friends, the family in the kayak: 'Wait for me, I'd like to make some dried fish.'

All these people are living in a camp by this lake, which is already free of ice in June. The fishing has been good. To mark the success one man has built an inuksuk and carved a tukipqutaq for the top, which looks like the face and arm of an inuk (person) pointing to the good fishing. On the arm he has hung a drying fish. Meanwhile his son is hunting from behind a blind of rocks they have built for watching the caribou.

The family in the kayak have caught many fish, while another couple have just left the kayak to walk ashore, the man carrying his wife to keep her dry. It is such a happy, lucky time that no one except the young boy in the kayak is afraid of the naqturalik (eagle). People used to believe— and some people still think maybe it is true—that these big birds would sometimes take people up and fly far away. The people would never come back. So they were scared of the naqturalik.

But these people are safe. Their friend the nanuq is going to catch the big bird. A happy camp in the springtime is a lucky place.

THE FRIENDLY FISH

A long time ago people lived in harmony with the animals, birds, and fish. They were so close that it seemed like the animals understood Inuktitut. In those days there was a great hunter named Kiviuq, who talked to a large fish and taught it to help people when they needed to get across the water but had no boat. It is difficult to know what Kiviuq should look like, so I have not drawn him. But these people have learned from him that the fish can carry them across a river. The birds, too, are helping. The people are travelling over the land to find a new camp where there is food.

In this drawing the fish is carrying the people. In real life it was often the fish that kept people alive in difficult times.

WOMAN SINGING

Two families are sharing their spring camp. Into their midst has wandered a stranger, the man in the purple atigi. He is from somewhere far away. It is a happy time, as spring usually is. One couple, both shamans, are expressing their happiness with a drum dance and song. They are supported on top of flowers, the form their shaman's spirits have taken. While he beats his caribou-skin drum and dances, she is singing, remembering her first successful hunt many years ago when she killed a wolf and a bird—a day she has never forgotten.

While they celebrate, their two sons have gone out of camp to hunt. They found a nanuq. The first arrow struck the bear, injuring it slightly. The second arrow broke. But they have more arrows. Nanuq will be theirs.

The stranger in camp is watching the dance, delighted because he has never before seen a drum dance. How lucky he feels to have arrived in camp today. The other couple in camp are watching too. He just caught a fish. His wife, smoking a pipe, is calling to her son to bring her ulu so that she can cut up the fish.

People are happy to be outside in the spring.

SUCCESSFUL HUNT

These families are travelling downriver to a new camp in early summer. The smaller kayaks each bear a family, fishing as they go. On the largest kayak, with a seal tied to the bow, a couple and two of their sons are waiting for their eldest son to join them. He went off hunting with one of the men the day before. They have returned with success. The man is carrying a caribou, wrapped in the skin— meat for everyone in the party who waited patiently by the river while the hunters were away. Now their journey may continue in comfort, to a destination unknown.

REGIONAL   RUTH TULURIALIK

THE LAND GAVE THE PEOPLE
LOTS OF FOOD

There were always times of good hunting, when the land
gave the people lots of food: nanuit, tuktu, seals, walrus,
birds and fish. Several families are hunting different things.
A magic ukpik (owl) watches.

SUMMER TRAVEL

Travelling to a summer camp was sometimes done by foot and sometimes by kayak. Often travellers would meet other travellers and make camps along the way.

One family travelling downriver is moving quickly with the current. The man wearing a red atigi is in the lead, with his wife and son following, each enjoying good fishing with their kakivak.

Another group is moving slowly upstream, just past a camp where a family of six lives in their caribou-skin tent. The family walking along the riverbank—mother, father, son, and dogs—have walked for miles and miles across the tundra. They are happy to see the family in camp and stop to visit. The family have given them a new puppy. Though the rest was welcome, they are soon on their way again.

Sometimes people just stopped to drink some tea, then left right away.

HAPPY HEARTS

This is a camp of friendly people who are happy because there are lots of caribou. Their hearts are soaring with happiness. Two of the men are at the caribou crossing, shooting the animals as they near shore. Another couple want to join the hunt, but tipped over their kayak in the excitement. Others are on their way to the hunt, or thinking of the meat they will get.

REGIONAL ᐱᓂᕐᒧᐊᕐᓂᖅ
RUTH TULURIALIK

DRUM DANCE

Maybe once during an entire summer the hunt was so successful the family had to celebrate with a qilaujaniq. While the hunter danced and beat his caribou-skin drum, his wife chanted her pissiq (song).

It is an evening in late spring. The snow has melted off the land, but the lakes are still frozen. The family is waiting for the open water so they can travel. The past two days were the best hunting they have had for years. In that short time, the father, in the purple atigi, caught two wolves, some fish, a bird, a polar bear, a rabbit, and a musk-ox. So he dances while his kneeling wife sings 'Ai ya ya . . . ai ya ya . . . ya ya' and repeats the names of the animals killed, in thanks. The oldest son, behind his father, cries out to his mother saying 'Don't forget the musk-ox!' All four sons join in. Even the youngest child, a daughter in her mother's amauti, seems to understand that something special is happening.

Another family arrived at this camp today—a man, his wife, and their son wearing a child's kyppak (kind of parka), made of caribou skin, fur out, drawn in at the waist. At their old camp they had no food, so they moved to the camp of their friends, who had lots of food. They have joined in the celebration with a drum dance of their own because earlier in the day the man killed a polar bear for the first time in his life.

FALL CAMP

It is September. Three days ago the man of this camp caught a caribou. He has returned to the hunt now. But before he left he built a cache for the meat, to save it till spring, and marked it with a small inuksuk. His wife is standing beside the cache, happy to see it. Their son is chasing a bird. And his grandmother is soon to use her ulu to cut up a seal. Behind her is the grandfather who died last month, laid upon the ground, his grave marked simply by a ring of stones.

All around them are the tools of their survival: the harpoon used to hunt seal, an auladjut for jigging fish, bow and arrow, kakivak for spearing fish, ice chisel and scoop, drum and beater, qataq (caribou-skin water bucket) and dipper, iqtuqsit (scraper), and on the fireplace a large tin pot they got by trading fox skins. The pot is ready to cook some caribou. They sometimes cooked all the parts, including the head and tongue, all day long to make them soft. The feet make a good soup. Only the antlers are not good to eat, but they are useful for other things. The water will soon be hot, ready for the hunter when he returns with his fresh meat.

WOMAN CARRYING WILLOW

In the camps women worked hard all the time, summer and winter. This woman is carrying a bundle of dry willow she has cut with her ulu. It will be used for a fire to make tea, or put under the caribou-skin sleeping mats to make the bed softer and warmer. The two grizzlies have frightened her. She is a long way from camp, out of sight.

In camp a family of nanuit have scared the people. One man is comforting his wife and mother. Another family is shooting at the mother bear—the son has landed one arrow and the father is readying another. Soon peace will be restored to this camp, the other woman will return with fuel, tea will be made, and life will continue.

IMAGINATION TENT

Early one September morning a young couple come out of their caribou-skin tent. They look around at the new day and see a musk-ox that has walked into their camp beside the sea. What good luck if they could kill it! With no children yet, and only one dog, a musk-ox would give them enough meat maybe for a whole year. While their dog barks at the musk-ox, they take up their bows and arrows, made of caribou bone and sinew, and begin the hunt.

Just as this is happening a father and his son, about 14, come by in two kayaks with their travelling companions: a dog and three geese. They have been travelling for five days since they left their own camp, hunting almost all the time, day and night. But they found no caribou. The son did most of the work. This was his father's way to teach him the skills of a hunter. Now he is so tired he is nearly asleep in his kayak. So he does not see the musk-ox on the shore. But his father does, and joins in the hunt with his friends in camp. His first arrow misses, but he has more inside his kayak.

The four faces on the tent are not real people yet. They are the children that will come to the young couple in the years ahead. They will have first a son, then a daughter, then another son, and last another daughter.

This story comes from a long time ago, before rifles and qablunat food, when children worked very hard to learn things they needed to know in order to live. That was the old Inuit way, before schools came here.

BAD POLICEMAN

In 1954 the RCMP were always watching for people going out hunting. They said the hunters should not kill any more caribou because it was the spring season. When they saw a boat leaving they chased after it to take away the guns. There were lots of caribou across the lake.

I remember one day some boats left very early, probably while the RCMP were sleeping. But my father and mother, Thomas and Elizabeth Tapatai, along with young David Annanowt and old Saqpuq, were later getting away. So the RCMP went after them. One man stood in the front of his boat and yelled 'STOP!'

I watched this from the shore, at our camp down by the Anglican mission, along with Deborah Niego, Lucy Tupik, and Salumi, an old woman who was visiting us. Lucy was looking forward to cutting up the caribou to make dried meat. But when I saw the policeman I thought: We will not have any caribou to eat after all. I would have nothing to eat but more biscuits.

The policemen were here to bring qablunat laws. The laws were supposed to protect us, they said, but this time they only hurt us.

THE 'BAY'

I remember when people used to come in from the land to trade at the Hudson's Bay post, about 1949. Very few of us lived here near the post. Most people lived out on the land, coming in to the Bay only once or twice a year, spring and fall—usually May and October when they could travel by dog teams. Normally the men came in from the camps by themselves, with their foxes, but sometimes they were accompanied by a few women.

Only at Christmas did whole families come in from the land. Then everybody stayed for the celebration. There were lots of iglus, all along the shore from the rock in front of the Bay to the Catholic mission, and many dogs.

In May the shelves in the Bay were nearly empty. There were no planes then. All the things came in on the ship in the summer. The people traded for biscuits, flour, baking powder, lard, tea, sugar, dried beans, molasses, cigarettes and tobacco, bullets, and rifles. They could get more for five foxes than we would get today for the money paid for five fox skins. The people pointed at what they wanted and the Bay manager took if off the shelf—not like today when we go around and pick things we want by ourselves. There was no heat in the building, so it was really freezing. The Bay manager just came over from his house when people arrived.

A man brings in one dried fox skin and two frozen foxes.

They used to trade both, but the dried skin was more valuable. There was an old Inuk working for the Bay manager to prepare all the skins from the frozen foxes. He worked very hard. Sometimes a hunter brought in 40 foxes at a time, which the old man had to skin, dry, and clean. The hunter's wife also brought some caribou clothing, which she made, to trade at the Bay.

In counting out the value of the skins, the Bay manager put some wooden tokens on the counter instead of money. The people will point out the things they want until all the wooden tokens are gone.

Another man and wife are just arriving at the Bay. He is carrying lots of foxes. His wife is following, thinking quietly about the box of biscuits she will get from the trader.

While these people have come in to the Bay, most of the people stayed out on the land, far away. In camp one woman is cooking a big pot of caribou soup over a fire built in the shelter of a skin, to block the wind. Several hungry people are waiting to eat. The rest of the camp is playing, enjoying themselves, except for one woman sitting off at the edge of camp chewing some caribou skin, to make it soft in preparation for some kamiik. They will all be happy when the people return from trading at the Bay, with a fresh supply of flour, tea, and other things.

It was a lot different even that short time ago.

THE MINISTER

When Christianity first came to Baker Lake in the early 1900s many people had trouble understanding, and some people wanted to stay with the beliefs they knew. Sometimes when people came in to trade at the Hudson's Bay post the minister would talk to them all. For most of these people it was the first time they ever saw a minister. For some, like the young boy pointing at the tall white man in his robes, it was the first time he had seen a qablunaq. Like the three people to one side of the minister, those who already know about God and Jesus sang the hymns happily.

When the minister said to the large group, 'I believe in God', some of them said 'Me too', but they did not really understand. The minister tried to explain to them; maybe after a year they began to understand. One man at the back of the group, who had trouble hearing, understood a little bit and was really happy. I remember seeing groups like this listening to the minister, usually in the church. But before the Anglican church at Baker Lake was built in 1930 they prayed outside, or sometimes the Hudson's Bay Company set up a big tent for the services in the summer.

The early ministers taught us to pray with our hands pressed flat together, fingers pointing up. That big hand represents the act of prayer, with the words coming out of the Bible: 'God so loved the world, he gave his only begotten Son, that whosoever shall believe in him, shall not perish but have eternal life.'

A long time ago, when the minister was preaching, some people—maybe praying very hard—could see a light glowing above his head. As a child you could really imagine it.

When I was young most people knew about religion because the early ministers here, Mr. Smith and Canon James, used to travel by dog-team out to the camps all around. They taught people in their camps, performed baptisms and marriages. My father, Thomas Tapatai, helped Canon James on these trips and in the settlement. The minister did everything: he was also the teacher, doctor, nurse, dentist, and adviser. I remember going to school with Canon James in his house. He used to tell us to go to bed early and to get up early, like we used to do in the camps. So when we saw him coming around at night we all ran to bed.

Lots of people used to come into the settlement from camps. I remember they gave some of their fox pelts to the church as an offering, before they traded the rest at the Hudson's Bay post. At Christmas and Easter many, many people came in, always carrying a lot of foxes. But when the new ministers came after Canon James they started to want more and more money instead of foxes. Sometimes it was hard to understand the ideas of religion.

Funny things happened when people did not really understand. One man, about to be baptized in the Roman Catholic church here, was going through the questions and responses to declare his faith. When asked what he was looking for from God, he answered: 'I want a new pair of pants.'

The ministers used to tell us not to go hunting on Sunday, so we never did. Even when there was really good fishing in springtime we had to be back by midnight on Saturday—when there was enough light to travel or fish all night. Now those people who work at steady jobs *only* hunt on Sundays, not like years before.

Many years ago, when there were only a few qablunat here, they taught us about religion. Now *we* have a committee to organize the church. We have our own choirs and catechists who also wear robes. We no longer see a light over the minister's head, nor give fox pelts as an offering. Very few of the 100 qablunat in the settlement come to church now. Things changed as the years went by.